Me | You

A 52 Week Guide Toward Making

Appreciation

Simple and Habitual at the Office

Trisha G. Harp, M.S., C.P.C

www.HarpFamilyInstitute.com

Me | You A 52 Week Guide Toward Making Appreciation Simple and Habitual at the Office

Trisha G. Harp, M.S., C.P.C.

Find us on the World Wide Web at

http://www.HarpFamilyInstitute.com

Copyright © 2017 by Harp Family Institute

ISBN 978-1-387-25621-1
9 781387256211
Version 1.4

For everyone

Changing the Golden Rule to the Platinum Rule

Like so many others, I was taught the Golden Rule when I was growing up. The meaning of "Do unto other as you would have them do unto you" seemed clear enough: treat others as you would want to be treated.

So I did. I tried to treat others with the kindness and respect that I sought from others, as the Golden Rule insisted. But after a while, I also noticed a big problem with this popular guiding principle. Often, what I was doing for others didn't match up with what I would want if the situation were reversed. I don't particularly care for Thank You notes and I don't need more trinkets from people, but according to the Golden Rule, that would mean I shouldn't give them to others, either. But the truth is other people really value them.

Sure enough, after over a decade of doing my own proprietary research, collecting data, interviewing people, coaching men, women, and couples, one thing has become crystal clear: the Golden Rule isn't always golden. Quite the opposite. If we really want to give to others, we shouldn't treat them as we want to be treated. We should treat them as *they* want to be treated.

I like to call this the Platinum Rule! As individuals, we experience and receive love and appreciation in our own unique ways. What is meaningful to one person might not impact another in the same way. In my research on how marriage and entrepreneurship intertwine, the disconnect that kept cropping up between the couples I researched was due to the fact that they hadn't communicated enough with one another. They had not discussed what they wanted and how they would like to be treated.

Although you are in an office setting, the same principals of appreciation and gratitude apply. *Research shows that when a business incorporates a value-based recognition system—a program that specifies ways to show appreciation for its employees' work and contributions—there is less turnover, higher employee engagement, and an increase in the bottom line.*

The goal of this book is to open the lines of communication between you and the individuals you work with on a daily basis. As you proceed through the year, think about what is most meaningful to you, to your co-workers and even to your boss. Do you enjoy things that make you laugh, sentimental trinkets or notes, interest in your personal life or are a smile and nod enough to bring you joy?

My hope for you is to increase your "bottom line" both at home and at your office by becoming more aware of how those in your life want to be treated—and then acting on that awareness. This year of exercises is also for you to learn about yourself and how you want to be treated.

Many of these tasks may feel awkward or contrived at first. That's ok. The idea is that a year from now, you will all be able to express appreciation toward one another in the way your fellow co-workers enjoy it the most. After you have committed to really learning about yourself and those around you, doing for others should become simple and habitual.

Promissory Note to Each Other

- I promise to do (or at least try) to do the weekly task.
- I promise to take this challenge seriously.
- I promise to commit to doing this for as long as my company and co-workers want to continue.
- I promise to laugh and have fun with this!

Have everyone who wishes to participate sign this page.

How this works:

1. Keep this book somewhere everyone will see it daily. (ie: staff room etc.)

2. Choose the day of the week to read the task. You may want to do it during the week. In this case, you would read it on Monday and complete it by Friday. Another option is to include weekends so you have more time to complete the task. In that case, you may choose to read the task on Friday and have it completed by the following Friday.

3. Weekly pairings are done like speed dating. Depending on how many people you have in your office, split the group into two. (If you have an odd number, one group will have 3 people in it.) Write the names in two columns. The column on the left stays put. The column on the right goes down one name each week. The bottom name circles back up to the top.

4. Everyone in the office will have the same task. Be creative and thoughtful on how you choose to execute on your task. It's ok to ask your partner if they have a preference about something. That's

part of the Platinum Rule!

5. You have 1 week to complete your task.

6. After your partner has completed their task, use the following sentence to convey how you felt about the task (not necessarily about their execution of it). Do this prior to your weekly staff meeting.

   Thank you so much for _____. I really liked _____ about it. I would rate the task ___ stars (1-5). It made me feel _____ because _____. *or* I really didn't like the task because _____.

7. During your weekly staff meeting, set aside 5 minutes for 2 people to share their experience with the team.

8. Have fun with this!

List of participants

Stays the same	Rotates each week

To make this process easier, someone may need to convert this into a dynamic spreadsheet.

Example Page:

Week 1
Take a post-it note (or 2) and complete the following sentence: I really admire _____ about you because _____. Put it somewhere your partner will find it.

Rate the Task
Thank you so much for the <u>message.</u> I really liked <u>finding it on my computer</u>. I would rate the task <u>4.0</u> stars because <u>knowing that you admire my sense of humor made me smile.</u>

Rate the Task
Thank you so much for the <u>message.</u> I really liked <u>your handwriting</u>. I would rate the task <u>1.0</u> stars because <u>getting compliments makes me feel uncomfortable.</u>

Week 1

Take a post-it note (or 2) and complete the following sentence:

I really admire _____ about you because _____.

Put it somewhere your weekly partner will find it.

Rate the Task

Thank you so much for _____. I really liked _____ about it. I would rate the task _____ stars (1-5). It made me feel _____ because _____ *or* I really didn't like the task because _____.

Week 2

Ask your weekly partner about their favorite candy bar. Surprise them with it one day this week.

Rate the Task

Thank you so much for _____. I really liked _____ about it. I would rate the task _____ stars (1-5). It made me feel _____ because _____ or I really didn't like the task because _____.

Week 3

Compliment your weekly partner on something you noticed they did to make your workplace better.

Rate the Task

Thank you so much for _____. I really liked _____ about it. I would rate the task _____ stars (1-5). It made me feel _____ because _____ *or* I really didn't like the task because _____.

Week 4

Ask you weekly partner to tell you something about their family life that you may not already know.

Rate the Task

Thank you so much for _____. I really liked _____ about it. I would rate the task _____ stars (1-5). It made me feel _____ because _____ or I really didn't like the task because _____.

Week 5

Ask your weekly partner about their favorite culinary flavor. Bring them something that relates to their answer.

Rate the Task

Thank you so much for _____. I really liked _____ about it. I would rate the task _____ stars (1-5). It made me feel _____ because _____ or I really didn't like the task because _____.

Week 6

Complete the following sentence on a card
or piece of paper:
I really like working with you because:
When you're done, give the paper to your weekly
partner.

Rate the Task

Thank you so much for _____. I really liked
_____ about it. I would rate the task _____ stars
(1-5). It made me feel _____ because _____ or
I really didn't like the task because _____.

Week 7

Come up with 1 joke to share with your weekly partner. Memorize it and deliver it without notes.

Rate the Task

Thank you so much for _____. I really liked _____ about it. I would rate the task _____ stars (1-5). It made me feel _____ because _____ *or* I really didn't like the task because _____.

Week 8

Take a series of goofy selfies with your weekly partner. Choose your favorite one together and post it somewhere in the office.

Rate the Task

Thank you so much for _____. I really liked _____ about it. I would rate the task _____ stars (1-5). It made me feel _____ because _____ or I really didn't like the task because _____.

Week 9

Find out your weekly partners preferred coffee/tea/drink. Bring it in for them one day.

Rate the Task

Thank you so much for _____. I really liked _____ about it. I would rate the task _____ stars (1-5). It made me feel _____ because _____ or I really didn't like the task because _____.

Week 10

Help your weekly partner clean up something. It could be lunch, their work space, filing, the conference room etc. Be creative and don't clean something for them; do it together.

Rate the Task

Thank you so much for _____. I really liked _____ about it. I would rate the task _____ stars (1-5). It made me feel _____ because _____ *or* I really didn't like the task because _____.

Week 11

Ask your weekly partner to share with you a cherished memory from their childhood.

Rate the Task

Thank you so much for _____. I really liked _____ about it. I would rate the task _____ stars (1-5). It made me feel _____ because _____ *or* I really didn't like the task because _____.

Week 12

Go to the Dollar Store and spend $1 on something you think your weekly partner will enjoy.

Rate the Task

Thank you so much for _____. I really liked _____ about it. I would rate the task _____ stars (1-5). It made me feel _____ because _____ *or* I really didn't like the task because _____.

Week 13

On a piece of paper, let your weekly partner know one thing you think makes them awesome at their job.

Rate the Task

Thank you so much for _____. I really liked _____ about it. I would rate the task _____ stars (1-5). It made me feel _____ because _____ or I really didn't like the task because _____.

Week 14

Have a staring contest with your weekly partner.

Rate the Task

Thank you so much for _____. I really liked
_____ about it. I would rate the task _____ stars
(1-5). It made me feel _____ because _____ *or*
I really didn't like the task because _____.

Week 15

Make plans to have lunch with your weekly partner this week.

Rate the Task

Thank you so much for _____. I really liked _____ about it. I would rate the task _____ stars (1-5). It made me feel _____ because _____ *or* I really didn't like the task because _____.

Week 16

Ask your weekly partner the following question. What can I do for you this week to make your life a little easier? Then follow through.

Rate the Task

Thank you so much for _____. I really liked _____ about it. I would rate the task _____ stars (1-5). It made me feel _____ because _____ *or* I really didn't like the task because _____.

Week 17

Give your weekly partner a high five every time you see them this week. Say, "you rock" each time you high five each other.

Rate the Task

Thank you so much for _____. I really liked _____ about it. I would rate the task _____ stars (1-5). It made me feel _____ because _____ *or* I really didn't like the task because _____.

Week 18

Ask your weekly partner to tell you a story related their favorite sports team.

Rate the Task

Thank you so much for _____. I really liked _____ about it. I would rate the task _____ stars (1-5). It made me feel _____ because _____ or I really didn't like the task because _____.

Week 19

Find out your weekly partner's favorite hobby. Do or buy something for them related to their answer.

Rate the Task

Thank you so much for _____. I really liked _____ about it. I would rate the task _____ stars (1-5). It made me feel _____ because _____ *or* I really didn't like the task because _____.

Week 20

Pull a practical joke on your weekly partner.

Rate the Task

Thank you so much for _____. I really liked _____ about it. I would rate the task _____ stars (1-5). It made me feel _____ because _____ or I really didn't like the task because _____.

Week 21

Write down 5 words that best describe your weekly partner and give it to them.

Rate the Task

Thank you so much for _____. I really liked _____ about it. I would rate the task _____ stars (1-5). It made me feel _____ because _____ *or* I really didn't like the task because _____.

Week 22

Have a thumb war with your weekly partner. Actually say the words, "One, two, three, four, let's have a thumb war."

Rate the Task

Thank you so much for _____. I really liked _____ about it. I would rate the task _____ stars (1-5). It made me feel _____ because _____ *or* I really didn't like the task because _____.

Week 23

Commit to making your bed every day this week.
Check in on your weekly partner to see if they followed
through each day. Ask each other if it makes a
difference for them.

Rate the Task

Thank you so much for _____. I really liked
_____ about it. I would rate the task _____ stars
(1-5). It made me feel _____ because _____ or
I really didn't like the task because _____.

Week 24

Go for a 10 minute walk with your weekly partner this week. Even if it's just walking around the office for 10 minutes.

Rate the Task

Thank you so much for _____. I really liked _____ about it. I would rate the task _____ stars (1-5). It made me feel _____ because _____ *or* I really didn't like the task because _____.

Week 25

Ask your weekly partner to teach you something you think they do well at work.

Rate the Task

Thank you so much for _____. I really liked _____ about it. I would rate the task _____ stars (1-5). It made me feel _____ because _____ *or* I really didn't like the task because _____.

Week 26

Make a list of the top 5 things you are grateful for.
Share your list with your weekly partner.

Rate the Task

Thank you so much for _____. I really liked
_____ about it. I would rate the task _____ stars
(1-5). It made me feel _____ because _____ or
I really didn't like the task because _____.

Week 27

Ask your weekly partner about their favorite snack.
Bring it in for them this week.

Rate the Task

Thank you so much for _____. I really liked
_____ about it. I would rate the task _____ stars
(1-5). It made me feel _____ because _____ or
I really didn't like the task because _____.

Week 28

Come up with a cool or secret handshake with your weekly partner.

Rate the Task

Thank you so much for _____. I really liked _____ about it. I would rate the task _____ stars (1-5). It made me feel _____ because _____ *or* I really didn't like the task because _____.

Week 29

Find a book that you have read and enjoyed. Give a copy to your weekly partner and tell them why you think they should read it.

Rate the Task

Thank you so much for _____. I really liked _____ about it. I would rate the task _____ stars (1-5). It made me feel _____ because _____ or I really didn't like the task because _____.

Week 30

Search for a Coke© with your weekly partner's name on it. If you can't find one, buy one with the closest name you can find and give it to them.

Rate the Task

Thank you so much for _____. I really liked _____ about it. I would rate the task _____ stars (1-5). It made me feel _____ because _____ *or* I really didn't like the task because _____.

Week 31

Come up with a #hashtag that best describes your weekly partner and share it with them.

Rate the Task

Thank you so much for _____. I really liked _____ about it. I would rate the task _____ stars (1-5). It made me feel _____ because _____ *or* I really didn't like the task because _____.

Week 32

Do a palm reading for your weekly partner. Make it up and be creative.

Rate the Task

Thank you so much for _____. I really liked _____ about it. I would rate the task _____ stars (1-5). It made me feel _____ because _____ *or* I really didn't like the task because _____.

Week 33

Find out about your weekly partner's favorite sports team. Look up one fact about the team to talk with them about.

Rate the Task

Thank you so much for _____. I really liked _____ about it. I would rate the task _____ stars (1-5). It made me feel _____ because _____ *or* I really didn't like the task because _____.

Week 34

Identify a dialect to talk in with your weekly partner. Choose a "dialect day" and every time you are together that day, commit to speaking in your chosen dialect.

Rate the Task

Thank you so much for _____. I really liked _____ about it. I would rate the task _____ stars (1-5). It made me feel _____ because _____ *or* I really didn't like the task because _____.

Week 35

Ask your weekly partner the following question: Who is the one person in your life that makes you the happiest and why?

Rate the Task

Thank you so much for _____. I really liked _____ about it. I would rate the task _____ stars (1-5). It made me feel _____ because _____ or I really didn't like the task because _____.

Week 36

Buy your weekly partner a new set of their favorite pens or desk accessory.

Rate the Task

Thank you so much for _____. I really liked _____ about it. I would rate the task _____ stars (1-5). It made me feel _____ because _____ or I really didn't like the task because _____.

Week 37

Ask your weekly partner about their favorite animal. Do something for them somehow related to that animal.

Rate the Task

Thank you so much for _____. I really liked _____ about it. I would rate the task _____ stars (1-5). It made me feel _____ because _____ *or* I really didn't like the task because _____.

Week 38

Every time you see your weekly partner give them a fist bump. With each fist bump, say, "Yo!"

Rate the Task

Thank you so much for _____. I really liked _____ about it. I would rate the task _____ stars (1-5). It made me feel _____ because _____ or I really didn't like the task because _____.

Week 39

Buy your weekly partner a small desktop gift you think they will like. For example, a small zen garden, a mini putting green or a quote block. Spend no more than $10.

Rate the Task

Thank you so much for _____. I really liked _____ about it. I would rate the task _____ stars (1-5). It made me feel _____ because _____ *or* I really didn't like the task because _____.

Week 40

Before you leave the office one day this week, write one reason your weekly partner rocks on the white board / message board at your office.

Rate the Task

Thank you so much for _____. I really liked _____ about it. I would rate the task _____ stars (1-5). It made me feel _____ because _____ or I really didn't like the task because _____.

Week 41

Have a coffee / drink with your weekly partner inside or outside of the office.

Rate the Task

Thank you so much for _____. I really liked _____ about it. I would rate the task _____ stars (1-5). It made me feel _____ because _____ *or* I really didn't like the task because _____.

Week 42

Make something out of paper clips to give to your weekly partner.

Rate the Task

Thank you so much for _____. I really liked _____ about it. I would rate the task _____ stars (1-5). It made me feel _____ because _____ *or* I really didn't like the task because _____.

Week 43

Find a photograph that includes you. Share it with your weekly partner and explain why it is meaningful to you.

Rate the Task

Thank you so much for _____. I really liked _____ about it. I would rate the task _____ stars (1-5). It made me feel _____ because _____ *or* I really didn't like the task because _____.

Week 44

Give your weekly partner a hug (or a handshake if hugs are strictly off limits).

Rate the Task

Thank you so much for _____. I really liked _____ about it. I would rate the task _____ stars (1-5). It made me feel _____ because _____ or I really didn't like the task because _____.

Week 45

Pretend this week is your weekly partner's birthday. Do something fun for them and help them celebrate!

Rate the Task

Thank you so much for _____. I really liked _____ about it. I would rate the task _____ stars (1-5). It made me feel _____ because _____ *or* I really didn't like the task because _____.

Week 46

Find an article online you think your weekly partner would enjoy and send it to them.

Rate the Task

Thank you so much for _____. I really liked _____ about it. I would rate the task _____ stars (1-5). It made me feel _____ because _____ *or* I really didn't like the task because _____.

Week 47

Ask your weekly partner about their favorite movie. Sometime during the week, say a line from that movie at a funny, but appropriate time.

Rate the Task

Thank you so much for _____. I really liked _____ about it. I would rate the task _____ stars (1-5). It made me feel _____ because _____ *or* I really didn't like the task because _____.

Week 48

Ask you weekly partner who they learned the most from in their lives regarding the work you currently do. Have them share 1 of the lessons they learned.

Rate the Task

Thank you so much for _____. I really liked _____ about it. I would rate the task _____ stars (1-5). It made me feel _____ because _____ or I really didn't like the task because _____.

Week 49

Write a 4-line poem or limerick to your weekly partner. Roses are red and Dr. Suess inspired lyrics are allowed.

Rate the Task

Thank you so much for _____. I really liked _____ about it. I would rate the task _____ stars (1-5). It made me feel _____ because _____ or I really didn't like the task because _____.

Week 50

Go to the Dollar Store and find a hat (or article of clothing) to give to your weekly partner. Commit to wearing it for at least 1 hour this week and to our staff meeting.

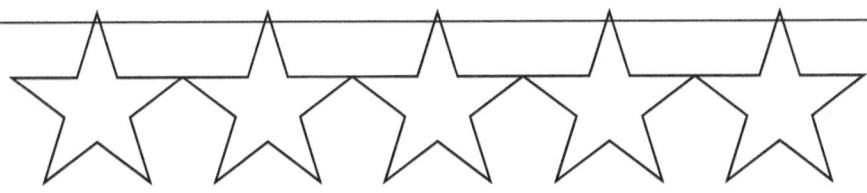

Rate the Task

Thank you so much for _____. I really liked _____ about it. I would rate the task _____ stars (1-5). It made me feel _____ because _____ *or* I really didn't like the task because _____.

Week 51

Identify your 5 favorite tasks from the year. Share them with your weekly partner and tell them why they were your favorites.

Rate the Task

Thank you so much for _____. I really liked _____ about it. I would rate the task _____ stars (1-5). It made me feel _____ because _____ *or* I really didn't like the task because _____.

Week 52

During your next staff meeting, share your previous weekly partner's 5 favorite tasks and share what they liked about them. Have a note taker write down each person's favorites in a notebook / computer for everyone in the office to reference.

Rate the Task

Thank you so much for _____. I really liked _____ about it. I would rate the task _____ stars (1-5). It made me feel _____ because _____ *or* I really didn't like the task because _____.

www.ingramcontent.com/pod-product-compliance
Lightning Source LLC
Chambersburg PA
CBHW021911170526
45157CB00005B/2047